Thomas Edison

Great Inventor

Mitchell Lane
PUBLISHERS

P.O. Box 196
Hockessin, Delaware
19707

Titles in the Series

Visit us on the web: www.mitchelllane.com
Comments? email us: mitchelllane@mitchelllane.com

Scientific Advancements of the 19th Century

Thomas Edison
Great Inventor

by Rebecca Thatcher Murcia

Scientific Advancements of the 19th Century

Mitchell Lane
PUBLISHERS

Printing   1   2   3   4   5   6   7   8

Library of Congress Cataloging-in-Publication Data

Murica, Rebecca Thatcher, 1962-
    Thomas Edison : great inventor / Rebecca Thatcher Murcia.
        p. cm. — (Uncharted, unexplored, and unexplained)
    Includes bibliographical references and index.
    ISBN 1-58415-306-7 (library bound)
    1. Edison, Thomas A. (Thomas Alva), 1847-1931—Juvenile literature. 2. Inventors—United States—Biography—Juvenile literature. 3. Electric engineers—United States—Biography—Juvenile literature. I. Title. II. Series.
TK140.E3M837 2004
621.3'092—dc22

                                                                    2004002050

ABOUT THE AUTHOR: Rebecca Thatcher-Murcia grew up in Garrison, New York, and graduated from the University of Massachusetts at Amherst. Murcia was a daily newspaper reporter—mostly in Texas—for 14 years. She lives in Akron, Pennsylvania, with her husband and two sons. She is the author of several books for young adults, including *Americo Paredes* and *Dolores Huerta* (Mitchell Lane).

PHOTO CREDITS: Cover, pp. 1, 3, 41—Photo Researchers; pp. 8, 16, 26, 34—Hulton Archive; pp. 6, 8, 18, 20, 26, 32, 34, 38, 40—Corbis; pp. 14, 23, 40—Library of Congress, pp. 12, 25, 36—General Electric; p. 10—Edison National Historic Site; p. 28—Bettmann Archive.

PUBLISHER'S NOTE: This story is based on the author's extensive research, which she believes to be accurate. Documentation of such research is contained on page 47.

The internet sites referenced herein were active as of the publication date. Due to the fleeting nature of some web sites, we cannot guarantee they will all be active when you are reading this book.

Thomas Edison

Great Inventor

Thomas Edison had little formal education but became one of history's most prolific and important inventors. Using his most self-taught scientific knowledge, he invented the light bulb, the phonograph, and the motion picture.

1

Recording a Miracle

Late in 1877, Thomas Edison drew a sketch of his idea for a new invention. He handed the sketch to John Kruesi, one of the finest machinists and craftsman working at Edison's company in New Jersey.

When Kruesi was almost finished building the machine, he asked Edison what on earth it was for.

"The machine must talk,"[1] Edison answered.

Kruesi could not believe his ears. A talking machine? The concept seemed absurd.

Kruesi kept working and finished the contraption. It was made of brass and iron and had a cylinder attached to a foot-long shaft. There were two diaphragms, or sound receivers, each with a needle at the end.

On December 6, 1877, Kruesi and other workers gathered around the new machine. Edison put a sheet of tinfoil around one cylinder, began turning the handle and sang "Mary Had a Little Lamb." The little machine scratched out a pattern on the tinfoil. Edison then put the needle back to the beginning of the recorded scratches, and turned the handle.

Everyone was shocked when Edison's voice came back out of the machine, singing "Mary Had a Little Lamb." Kruesi, who had built the machine, was especially surprised. The color drained from his face and he exclaimed in his native German.

"I was never so taken aback in all my life. Everybody was astonished," Edison said. "I was always afraid of things that worked the first time."[2]

It was a momentous event in Edison's long life as an inventor, and, as he said, one of the few times that something worked more quickly than he had expected. Ironically, Edison did not begin making and selling the phonograph quickly. He was busy with other projects and could not imagine the huge recorded music industry that would grow up in the next century. Instead he thought the invention would be more useful as a business machine, like the increasingly successful typewriter.

But the phonograph, like the light bulb and the motion picture, would eventually take its place on the list of Edison's groundbreaking inventions. It would be one of the amazing changes in our society that Edison brought about during his long life as one of the world's foremost inventors.

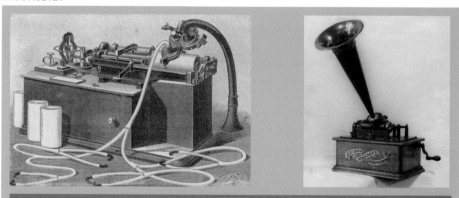

At first Thomas Edison saw the phonograph as a business machine. He thought secretaries could use the machine to record spoken comments, and then later play back the comments and type them into a typewriter. But that use of the phonograph never became very popular; many secretaries in the United States were trained in written shorthand that is useful for recording speech.

the Typewriter

It is no wonder that Edison imagined his phonograph first and foremost as a business machine. At the time, the American office was just beginning to undergo revolutionary changes.

In 1868, almost a decade before Edison invented the phonograph, three Americans— Samuel Soulé, Christopher Latham Sholes and Carlos Glidden—invented the first commercially successful typewriter. The three men contracted with Remington, a company that was already making sewing machines and rifles, to begin manufacturing their invention in 1873.

Other inventors had obtained patents for typewriters. The first was Henry Mill of Great Britain, who obtained a patent for a writing machine in 1714. But Soulé, Sholes, and Glidden were the first ones to design a machine that worked well enough to be manufactured and sold.

The new typewriters sold widely and quickly changing the way American companies did business. Letters, bills, lists, and other important business documents were produced neatly and more easily on the typewriter, instead of laboriously by hand. The Remington and the other early models that followed it were soon to be found in offices throughout the United States and in other countries.

One problem with the early typewriters was the tendency of the keys to jam up together if the writer was typing too quickly. For that reason, the QWERTY keyboard, named for the first six letters in the top row, was designed with letters positioned to prevent the typist from proceeding too quickly. Today, with computers used more extensively and typewriters almost obsolete, the original QWERTY keyboard is still in use even though other designs would be faster.

The invention of the typewriter was part of the Industrial Revolution that changed American society in the 19th and 20th centuries. The United States— especially in the north—was gradually transformed from a society in which the majority of the people worked on farms into the most advanced industrial nation on earth. The trend continued into the 20th century, when President Calvin Coolidge was quoted famously as saying, "The chief business of America is business."

Teachers complained that Thomas Edison could not sit still and pay attention, so his mother decided to teach him at home. At the age of 12, he began working, but he always maintained some sort of laboratory where he could study science and do experiments.

2

Growing Up Inventive

Thomas Alva Edison was born on February 11, 1847, in Milan, Ohio. His parents, Samuel and Nancy Edison, had moved to Milan from Canada ten years earlier. Samuel Edison had taken part in a rebellion against the government of Canada, which was still a colony of England. He had to flee across the border when it failed. Now he ran a shingle manufacturing business. Nancy Edison was the daughter of a Baptist minister. She had worked as a schoolteacher and was well educated for a woman of her time. When Thomas was born, Nancy Edison had already given birth to three sons—William Pitt, Carlisle, and Samuel Ogden II—and three daughters, Marion, Harriet Ann, and Eliza. But life was not easy for the children. The winters were harsh and the children suffered from colds and other illnesses. Carlisle died when he was six and Samuel II and Eliza both died as babies.

Thomas Edison was born during a heavy winter snowstorm, and was also often ill as a small child. As he grew up, he began constantly asking questions and wondering about all kinds of topics. His parents sent him to school, but he did not do well there. He had trouble sitting still and listening to the teacher. His mother decided to teach him at home. Her patience had its limits; she kept a stick behind the grandfather clock and Edison often said that she wore the bark off the stick thrashing him with it. Edison's home schooling was unconventional but successful in its own way. He read science books and performed experiments in his base-ment. But he always seemed to have a knack for getting in trouble. This continued after the family moved to a house on a military reservation in Port Huron, Michigan.

Nancy Elliott Edison and Samuel Edison

Once Thomas decided to find out if an older boy could fly if he drank enough gas-producing powder mixed with water. The boy did as Thomas told him, drank the mixture and became very ill. In another incident, Thomas went swimming in a creek with a friend. The other boy disappeared. For some reason, Thomas went home and went to bed instead of getting help. The next morning the boy's drowned body was pulled from the creek. Thomas was punished for his misadventures, but that did not slow him down.

As he grew older, he turned his energy into more positive directions. When he was 12, he began working on the nearby railroad. The train made a daily four-hour trip to Detroit. Thomas boarded the train and sold newspapers, vegetables from the family's garden, and other snacks to passengers during its trip. When the train reached Detroit, he had to wait several hours to return. He often went to the Detroit Public Library, where he read different types of non-fiction and literature.

Thomas especially enjoyed Victor Hugo's *Les Miserables*, a novel of the French Revolution. He said *The Age of Reason*, by Thomas Paine, was one of the most important books he read as a child. Thomas did not like church but had been forced to go and study the Bible. In Paine's writings, he found another world view that was based on modern democratic principles. "I can still remember the flash of enlightenment which shone from his pages," Edison recalled later. "It was a revelation, indeed, to encounter his views on political and religious matters, so different from the views of many people around us."[1] Paine also wrote *Common Sense*, a pamphlet that inspired the American colonialists' revolution against Britain.

Edison was always grateful to his mother for opening the world of literature and non-fiction books to him. "My mother taught me how to read good books quickly and correctly, and as this opened up a great world in literature, I have always been very thankful for this early training,"[2] he remarked.

Thomas was so impressed with the interest people had in news-papers that he decided to start his own. He bought a secondhand press and installed it in one of the freight cars on the train. At first he called his little newspaper *The Weekly Herald*. Later he changed the name to *Paul Pry* and he added more gossip and society news. But his career as a journalist ended when a man who had been mentioned in one of the columns threatened to throw Thomas into the St. Clair River.

Thomas Edison definitely had a rough-and-tumble boyhood, full of pranks and adventures. He began to lose his hearing as a boy, and often thought it was from one or two incidents. In one incident he was late for the train. He was running after it when a man reached down and picked him up by his ear. In another incident, a conductor reportedly beat his ears severely after some chemicals Edison had been storing on the train ignited and caused a fire. Doctors who examined his ears as an adult said he probably was born with a defect that may have been made worse by the injuries.

Even though he was a reliable worker earning a steady income, he still didn't lose his reputation as an adventurer and a wanderer and even a trickster. When the Civil War began in 1861, a regiment of Union soldiers was stationed at the fort near Thomas's house. There was a long line of sentinels, or guards, who kept watch over a large area during the night. These sentinels would pass information and messages up and down the line. Thomas and a friend started a message at the beginning of the line, calling the supervisor to the guard post. They did it for two nights in a row. On the third night, the soldiers were ready. They captured Thomas's friend, but Thomas ran home with the soldiers in hot pursuit. When the soldiers searched his house, he hid under some old potatoes in the basement.

He also caused trouble in little ways. The cats ran from him in terror because they were afraid he would use them to make static electricity. Thomas had always been fascinated by electricity and telegraphy.

He began to show what would become a lifelong talent as an entre-preneur when he used the telegraph to help sell newspapers during the Civil War. Edison noticed that when people were aware of a major Civil War battle, they bought more newspapers so they could find out the details about what happened. After the Battle of Shiloh in April 1862, he asked the telegraph operator at the station in Detroit to inform the stations along the route about the battle. He then asked the newspaper editor to give him 1,000 copies on credit. Big crowds gathered at each station, anxious to buy the newspaper. By the end of the route, he had raised the price to 25 cents and still sold all the papers.

The incident impressed him with the potential of telegraphy. But he didn't know how a person went from selling newspapers to working as a telegrapher. The opportunity, however, presented itself promptly.

Edison's family was fortunate not to have been directly affected by the suffering and death caused by the American Civil War. More than 600,000 soldiers were killed. Many thousands more died of diseases and injuries. The Civil War kept the United States together as a country, but it caused untold pain and suffering and opened conflicts that are still being argued about today.

The controversy that led to the Civil War grew slowly as the two regions of the United States—the North and the South—developed differently during the colonial period and the early 1800s. In the South, landowners formed large plantations, planted cotton, and bought slaves imported from Africa to care for the cotton and harvest it. The southern states exported the cotton to Europe and the North. While there were also farms in the North, they were not as big and they did not rely on slave labor. The North became a more industrial society, and was also more active in developing its roads and railroads.

Abraham Lincoln, who opposed slavery, was elected president in 1860. Leaders in the southern states feared he would outlaw slavery and decided to revolt. They formed the Confederate States of America and elected Jefferson Davis as president. The war started on April 12, 1861, when Confederate forces fired on Fort Sumter in Charleston, South Carolina.

The fighting continued for four years, much longer than anyone thought when it started. The North had more forces, especially with the help of slaves who escaped after Lincoln signed the Emancipation Proclamation in 1863. But the South only had to defend its territory, and it did so with great military leadership.

The war ended with the Confederate General Robert E. Lee's surrender on April 9, 1965. The celebration over the Northern victory was cut short when Lincoln was assassinated five days later. His stirring remarks at the consecration of the Civil War battlefield in Gettysburg, Pennsylvania, were one of the reasons he is remembered as one of the nation's greatest presidents.

Lincoln called on Americans to dedicate themselves to preserving a democratic form of government, "that this nation, under God, shall have a new birth of freedom—and that government of the people, by the people, for the people, shall not perish from the earth."

During long hours of work, study, and practice, Thomas Edison gained a thorough understanding of electricity and telegraphy. Later in his life, he used that knowledge to invent the phonograph.

3

Becoming an Inventor

On a summer day in 1862, Thomas was waiting for the train at the Mt. Clemens station. He noticed a three-year-old boy playing in the gravel on the main track. A train was bearing down on him. He raced to the boy, picked him up and pulled him out of the way just before the train arrived. The boy's father, James Mackenzie, was the stationmaster. He wanted to do something for the young man as a reward for saving his son's life. He remembered how much Edison liked telegraphy and offered to train him as a telegrapher. This was a great opportunity. Telegraphy was one of the fastest growing industries in the United States. Since the construction of the first telegraph line less than 20 years earlier, thousands of miles of telegraph wires and hundreds of telegraph stations had sprung up. Many telegraphers had gone off to fight in the Civil War. As a result, telegraphers were in short supply throughout the United States.

Edison spent five months working and training at the Mt. Clemens, Michigan station. He learned how to operate the telegraph equipment and how to send and receive messages in Morse code. Once he had mastered the basics, he took his first job as a part-time operator at the Port Huron station. Then, as in many subsequent times, his distractibility and his interest in science got him into trouble. He was doing an experiment with battery acid when the acid caused an explosion that broke

Thomas Edison was about 15 years old when he saved the life of a young boy who was playing along some train tracks. The boy's father volunteered to teach Edison Morse code and how to operate the telegraph machine. It was a great opportunity for Edison to learn more about what had always fascinated him: electricity.

glass and machinery in the office. He left Port Huron and found another job at Stratford Junction, Canada. One night he got a telegraphed order to hold a train so it wouldn't collide with another train coming in the opposite direction on the single track. The order came too late. The train he was supposed to hold had already departed. Fortunately the engineers on the trains saw each other's headlights and stopped just in time. Though it wasn't his fault, Thomas was blamed for the near disaster. When he heard railroad officials discussing possible punishments for him—including jail time—he fled back across the border to the United States.

Edison spent the next few years wandering the country, working as a telegrapher in one place for a few months and then moving on to another job. He could do the job well if he focused on it, but often he would be busy reading about science or doing an experiment with electricity. Sometimes he would just do things that would annoy his fellow workers, such as write out the telegraph messages in huge letters or in very tiny letters. He was always studying telegraph equipment, trying to figure out how it worked and how to make it work better. Edison recalled many years later that his discussions with other telegraph workers were often fruitless.

"The telegraph men couldn't explain how it worked, and I was always trying to get them to do so. I think they couldn't. I remember the best explanation I got was from an old Scotch line repairer employed by the Montreal Telegraph Company, which operated the railroad wires. He said that if you had a dog like a dachshund, long enough to reach from Edinburgh to London, if you pulled his tail in Edinburgh he would bark in London. I could understand that, but I never could get it through me what went through the dog or over the wire,"[1] he said.

These were trying times for his parents, who wondered if he would ever be a success in life. He always seemed to be drifting from job to job and from place to place.

In 1868, Edison wound up in Boston. The city, with a thriving economy and many excellent universities nearby, was a center of technological experimentation and invention. Edison came across a book by the renowned scientist Michael Faraday, *Experimental Researches in Electricity*. Finally, he was given a clear and understandable explanation of what scientists knew about electricity at the time. He also saw how Boston inventors set up shops with lots of tools and materials on which to work. After years of informal experiments and investigations, Edison was ready to begin to invent new technology and see how he could improve upon existing telegraphy. There were several difficulties with the telegraph equipment currently in use. One was that messages could only be transmitted about 200 miles. After 200 miles, they had to be re-written and re-transmitted. That was time-consuming and also introduced the possibility of error. Another problem was that messages could only be sent in one direction on the telegraph wires.

A shop owner let Edison use a little of his space so he could begin his experiments. Edison did not sleep much. He would work all night at

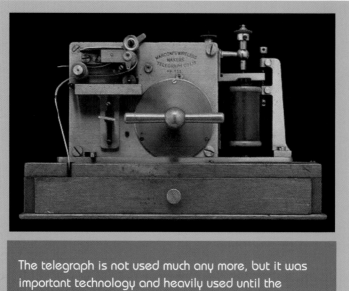

The telegraph is not used much any more, but it was important technology and heavily used until the telephone came along many years later. Even today, the word telegraph means the same thing as instantaneous communication.

the telegraph office and then work all day on his experiments, only taking quick naps in between. He knew more about electricity than he did in the past, but that did not prevent him from making mistakes. Once he grabbed a large induction coil with both hands. He found that his hands were frozen to the coil. The only way he could break the electrical connection was to lean back so the wires would pull the battery off the shelf, thus breaking the circuit. "I shut my eyes and pulled, but the nitric acid splashed all over my face and ran down my back. I rushed to the sink ... and got in as well as I could,"[2] Edison said. The acid from the batteries burned Edison's face and back.

Edison persisted, and in June 1868 he developed his first duplex telegraph. It could send messages in both directions at once. He did not seek a patent on that machine and would have to keep refining it. Edison was only 22 years old and had very little formal education. But he was skilled and knowledgeable. In January 1869 he announced that he would no longer work as a telegraph operator. Instead he would devote himself full-time to inventions. By June that year he received his first patent. It was for an electronic vote-counting machine. He enthusiastically took the machine to different state governments. He found that they were not interested in counting their votes electronically. He realized he would have to focus his creativity on inventions for which there was a more clearly established need.

He turned his efforts once again to improving telegraphy. He began refining his duplex telegraph machine. A businessman loaned him $500 to pay for the tools and equipment he needed. Edison persuaded the owners of the Atlantic & Pacific Telegraph Company in Boston to let him experiment over their network of wires. Filled with optimism, he left detailed instructions for an operator in Boston and took his machines and equipment to Rochester, New York, to begin testing his device. It didn't work. After a few days he returned to Boston to say that his idea had failed and that he could not repay the $500 loan.

Edison felt trapped. After the failure of the duplex machine, nobody in Boston would pay him to keep inventing. He owed money and had no results to offer his lender. In a move that could have been disastrous but ended up successfully, Edison borrowed a few dollars from a friend and went to New York City. He arrived hungry and homeless, determined to make a fresh start. He saw Franklin Pope, an electrical engineer and telegraph expert who worked for the Gold Indicator Company. The company was providing an important service. It informed gold and stock traders in the area around Wall Street and the New York Stock Exchange about changes in the price of gold, which could affect the financial markets. Although the telegraph technology the company used was fairly new and primitive, financial companies in the area were already relying on the way it quickly and efficiently distributed information. Pope, who had already heard a little about Edison, let the young man sleep in the company's cellar.

Shortly after Edison arrived, the machine that transmitted the price information jammed and stopped. Hundreds of messenger boys came running to the office from all the different companies the Gold Indicator Company served, demanding to know what had happened and how the gold prices had changed. Pope and S.S. Laws, the inventor of the machine, tried to figure out what had happened. But they could not find the problem. Edison examined it carefully. He found that a spring had broken off and become stuck between two gears. Soon he had retrieved the spring and fixed the machine. Laws and Pope were thrilled. They offered Edison a job maintaining and improving the machines.

The job was perfect. Edison could study and experiment with the equipment and earn a steady paycheck. He happily set to work finding the faults in the transmitter and improving it. He figured out how to make it print letters and numbers on paper. After just a few months, Edison was ready to take an even bigger step. When the company merged with another one to form the Gold & Stock Company, Edison and Pope struck out on their own. They formed an electrical engineering company just across the Hudson River in Jersey City, New Jersey. They offered their services as electrical and telegraph experts.

The head of the Gold & Stock Company, General Marshall Lefferts, asked Edison to study a stock printing machine the company owned and invent a way to keep it from "running wild" or printing random numbers and letters from time to time. Edison studied the problem and designed a switch that could stop the printers in other offices from the home office. He met with the owners of the company to show them his invention. Lefferts and the other owners were impressed and asked him how much they should pay him for his work. Edison hesitated, thinking that perhaps he should ask for as much as $4,000. Lefferts, seeing Edison hesitate, jumped in with an offer of $40,000. Edison was shocked and accepted the check on the spot. When he took it to the bank, the teller shouted something at him that he could not understand, so he returned to the company. A clerk with the company took him back to the bank, where they realized that the teller simply wanted to see identification before cashing such a large check.

Edison had always lived hand-to-mouth and he did not know what to do with so much money. He took it home to the rooming house in New

Jersey where he was living, where he stayed up all night afraid of being robbed. The next morning he took the money back to the bank and opened up an account. It was just the beginning of Edison's life as a wealthy man. He eventually learned more about accounts and money management, but it would never be something he enjoyed or handled especially well.

He kept working at designing and manufacturing new and improved telegraph printing machines. There was fierce competition in the business and Edison could sometimes play the different companies against each other. He would invent something for one company and then the other company would get nervous and ask him to invent something else.

Edison and Pope soon parted ways. Edison found an investor who was willing to spend $30,000 to build him a shop, called the American Telegraph Works. Edison then hired a number of employees. Two of the most important were John Kruesi, the machinist who later helped him with the phonograph, and Charles Batchelor. These two talented men would stay with him for many years.

Edison was focused on work and had never spent much time with women. But in the fall of 1871, he met Mary Stilwell, an attractive 16-year-old girl who worked at the Gold & Stock Company. Never one to waste time with niceties, one day soon after they began seeing each other Edison asked Mary if she would marry him the next week. She agreed and the two were married on Christmas Day, 1871. That afternoon, Edison went back to the office and began working, leaving his new bride alone in their new home. Hours passed, and someone finally asked Edison if he was going home. He asked, "What time is it?"[3] When he was told it was midnight, he said, "Is that so? I must go home then. I was married today."[4]

The couple went on a honeymoon in Boston and then Edison went back to work. He worked long hours and his young wife quickly became unhappy with her lonely existence. Her sister, Alice, came to live with them. Edison was able to provide Mary and their children, Marion, Thomas Jr. and William, with a comfortable lifestyle. But he never was

Edison wasted no time asking Mary Stilwell to marry him. They married on Christmas Day in 1871. With Edison's long hours of work, he never had time for Mary and his children. Mary became ill and died on August 9, 1884.

the attentive husband and father his family might have wanted. His first commitment was always to his work.

Over the next few years Edison worked on improving different types of telegraph machines. He also struggled a little financially. He was never great at bookkeeping and keeping track of money. When sales of his telegraph machines declined in 1873 because of bad economic times, people to whom he owed money sued him. The sheriff tried to collect on the debts by seizing his machines. But Edison persuaded the sheriff to wait and managed to pay off the debts.

In 1874 he perfected a quadruplex telegraph machine, which could send four messages at once. It was a great invention. In one report, the major telegraph company, Western Union, predicted that the machine could save the company $20 million over the course of 30 years.

One result of inventing the quadruplex was making Edison success-ful enough to design and build his own center for inventing and manufacturing. Exploring the area around Newark, New Jersey, he found Menlo Park, a small village along a rail line. He built a long two-story building near the railway. With his own new facilities and experienced employees, Edison was finally free to invent and experiment as much as he wanted.

New inventions are not always well received. When Alexander Graham Bell invented the telephone in 1876, one of Edison's fellow inventors, Elisha Gray, said he thought the telephone was interesting but that the technology would be proven to be useless. "Talking telegraphy is a beautiful thing from a scientific point of view. . . . But if you look at in a business light, it is of no importance. We can do more . . . with a wire now than with that method,"[5] Gray told his patent lawyer.

Edison's first major project after setting up shop at Menlo Park was improving Bell's telephone. The first telephone had two major problems. There was a lot of interference. It was sometimes hard to understand people's voices over the line. Also, one had to listen with one piece and speak into a receiver. Western Union asked Edison to study Bell's telephone and improve it. All through the winter of 1877 Edison experimented with the telephone and worked on ways to improve it. His work on the telephone soon led to the invention of the phonograph.

Edison's home at Menlo Park was modest. But his system of bringing together talented people and having them work on inventions was an important step in the history of American technological development.

Edison had a great imagination and was able to envision the uses of new technology better than most people. But even he had his blind spots. After he invented the phonograph, Edison, who was partially deaf and not very musical, said, "I don't want the phonograph sold for amusement purposes. It is not a toy. I want it sold for business purposes only."[6]

Edison's work on the telephone, the quadruplex and the phonograph began to earn him fame. Reporters from the major New York newspapers came to visit Menlo Park. They wrote glowing stories about Edison's genius as an inventor. Edison loved the attention and sometimes exaggerated his abilities and accomplishments to make it seem as if he was even smarter than he really was. Soon he earned the nickname, "the Wizard of Menlo Park." He was about to invent something that would make it seem as if he fully deserved the title.

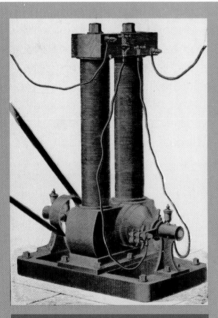

Edison improved the dynamo, a machine that generated electricity, to make it safer and less expensive. He later installed the first commercial system for electric light in the world in London and the first in the United States in New York City.

The kinetoscope was an early kind of moving picture machine. Only one person could see the film at a time, but the pictures and the sound were clearer than they were in the early projectors.

Samuel Morse and the Invention of the Telegraph

In 1775, the American Revolutionary Paul Revere made his famous ride through the towns around Boston, Massachusetts, warning his fellow patriots that the British were coming. Six decades later, most messages were still transmitted at the speed of a galloping horse, or about 15 miles per hour.

Electricians and inventors in Europe and the United States were studying the problem and trying to figure out how to use electricity to send messages. In 1837, Samuel Finley Breese Morse developed the telegraph machine, which could send electrical impulses over wires. Charles Wheatstone and William Cooke developed a similar machine in England the same year.

Morse also developed a system of code that could be used to translate short and long impulses into letters. In what became known as Morse code, for example, an A is a dot and a dash and a B is a dash and three dots.

In 1843 Morse persuaded the United States Congress to spend $30,000 putting up a telegraph line from Washington, D.C., to Baltimore, Maryland, about 40 miles away. When Morse tested the line for the first time the following year he sent the message, "What hath God wrought?" ("What has God done?"). Companies offering to telegraph messages from place to place sprang up all over the United States.

Hundreds of telegraph operators learned Morse code and went to work sending and receiving messages. The telegraph was especially a boon to newspapers, which used the telegraph services extensively to transmit news. Governments and businesses also used the telegraph to communicate information.

At first, many different telegraph companies competed against each other. They soon began merging and buying each other out until by the 1870s Western Union remained as the dominant telegraph company. After Alexander Graham Bell invented the telephone in 1876, telegraph and telephone services coexisted for many years. The telegraph eventually became obsolete. Western Union still exists today, but it now mostly moves money instead of transmitting messages.

Thomas Edison promised to invent an electric light that was moderate and steady, unlike the gas lamps and arc lights in use at the time. One British scientist said that Edison's promise showed that he knew next to nothing about electricity. Eventually Edison was successful, but the project was not as easy as he thought it would be.

4

Lighting up the World

In 1878, people used gas, oil, and candles to light their homes. Some cities had a type of electric lights that were known as arc lights. They were useful for lighting large spaces but the bulbs were far too bright to be useful in smaller settings such as homes and offices. Despite many efforts, no one had been able to think of a way to use electricity to light homes. Edison decided that he would be the one to conquer this problem. He knew a lot about electricity, and he was sure there was a way to design a light bulb for home use.

The obstacles were huge. It was a mystery how to make a steady, moderate light suitable for homes. Even if it had been, there was also no existing system to bring electricity into people's homes. Things taken for granted today, such as electric plugs connected to power supplies that come from power plants, simply did not exist. Edison would have to invent both a light bulb and an entire system for distributing the necessary electricity.

Edison's first problem was trying to figure out what would become incandescent, or glow, with an electric current inside a glass lamp or bulb. He needed a material that would provide the correct amount and intensity of light. Wires seemed to be possibilities, but they conducted electricity. Then it occurred to him that he needed something that would resist transmitting the current, or slow it down, instead of carrying it quickly. He tried many different kinds of materials. The gaslights of the day produced a carbon substance called lampblack on the inside of their glass shields. Edison was playing with some of the lampblack, kneading it between his thumb and forefinger, when it occurred to him that it might work in a light bulb. He strung a narrow strip of lampblack between two wires inside a light bulb and created a moderate light that burned for ten minutes. He knew he was on the right track. He called newspaper reporters and told them he would invent a long-lasting electric lamp quickly.

"There will be neither blaze nor flame, no singing or flickering; it will be white and steadier than any known lamp. It will give no obnoxious fumes nor smoke, will prove one of the healthiest lights possible, and will not blacken ceilings or furniture,"[1] Edison said.

At the time, these assertions seemed extraordinary, and were met with criticism from scientific experts. British scientist Silvanus P. Thompson said anyone who tried to invent an incandescent electric light was doomed to failure. Edison showed the "most airy ignorance of fundamental principles both of electricity and dynamics,"[2] Thompson wrote.

Edison would prove the experts wrong, but not as quickly as he originally thought. There were many obstacles Edison had to tackle before he could produce an electric lamp. He knew he had to improve the vacuum, or the absence of air, inside the bulb. But he didn't know how to remove the air completely. He heard that a man in England had invented a pump that could create excellent vacuums. One of these pumps was at nearby Princeton University. He sent Francis Upton, one of his assistants, to Princeton University to borrow the pump. Then he used it to remove the air from the inside of a light bulb with platinum wire inside. It worked a little better than previous attempts, but the platinum wire was not the right material.

Edison tried carbonized thread and paper, strung between platinum wires. In October 1879, he was able to keep one going for 15 hours. It burned with the same intensity as 30 candles. That was much better, but

Edison needed money to support this marathon of inventing. He found a new lawyer, Grosvenor Lowrey, who believed in Edison's brilliance as an inventor and also had good contacts in the New York financial world. Lowrey brought together a group of businessmen who agreed to finance the invention of the electric light bulb with an initial investment of $30,000. The businessmen were taking a risk. Experts of the day thought it was impossible to tame the frightening power of electricity and bring it into homes. Edison tended to exaggerate how quickly and inexpensively he would be able to do it. Over the next few years, Edison would go back to the same group of men for more money to pay for his research, while the goal of the electric light for every home seemed to remain far off.

But Edison worked tirelessly. He also assigned certain aspects of the project to highly qualified assistants whose work he supervised. By then he had 60 employees working at the laboratory. He would give one of his helpers a problem to solve, and encourage him to experiment freely. Edison asked Wilson Howell to figure out the best way to insulate electric wires underground. Howell spent two weeks in the library, reading books and articles about insulation, and then wrote a list of materials he wanted to try. He bought the materials he wanted to investigate and immediately began experimenting with different mixtures and formulas. "Of course there were many failures, the partial successes pointing the direction for better trials,"[3] Howell wrote.

By 1881 Edison had progressed enough to demonstrate his plans. On January 28 he strung up 425 lamps all around Menlo Park. He lit them for 12 hours using an electric dynamo—or generator—powered by a ton and a half of coal. Soon word of Edison's progress with the electric light spread and people began coming from all over to witness Edison's marvelous invention. The crowds would be thrilled to see Thomas Edison appear in his scruffy work clothes. He would regale them with incredible claims about how he would eventually light up the whole city of New York. Usually the people came to see Edison and Menlo Park and then left. A few visitors behaved badly, wandering into rooms that were supposed to be off limits and stealing some of the new electric lamps.

Edison was a great inventor and also a great showman. When word spread about his progress with electric lights, people began to come from miles around to see the miracle of the light bulb. Edison enjoyed being the center of attention but he also understood the importance of team work and hired experts in different scientific fields to help him with his inventions.

The next step was to set up an electricity generating station in New York City and supply the companies and households around Pearl Street in New York City with electricity and light bulbs. The project was successful, but Edison had still not achieved his goal of making electric lighting cheaply and easily available. The bulbs were still expensive to make. Accidents and injuries left some people wary of electricity.

Edison kept trying to find the ideal filament, the substance that would light up when electrified. He tested and examined thousands of different substances. He discovered one that worked the best almost by accident. He saw a bamboo fan, broke off a piece, and put it under his microscope. The fibers looked ideal for lighting up with electricity, and indeed they were. Edison ended up using bamboo in his lamps for several years before switching to a manufactured fiber. From 1880 to 1882, Edison either supervised or single-handedly investigated many different aspects of the electric system he needed in order to make lights that were safe and inexpensive enough for homes. Although some of the ideas and inventions were kept secret, Edison obtained patents for hundreds of inventions related to the electrical system.

In 1883, he discovered something that was not yet known about electricity. He noticed that there were tiny black spots on the inside of his lamps. He observed this phenomenon and called it a mystery. At that time scientists did not know that electric current involved the movement of electrons. These are tiny particles that rotate about the nucleus of atoms, the building blocks of every substance. Many years later, another scientist confirmed that the Edison Effect, as it was called, was actually the movement of electrons. This knowledge formed the basis of 20th century electronic inventions such as the television and the computer.

While Edison was dedicating his days and nights to inventing the system of electric lights that would change the world, his wife became ill. He pulled himself away from his work to go to her bedside, but she did not recover and died on August 9, 1884.

Edison's oldest daughter, Marion, remembered her father waking her up to tell her the news. "I found him shaking with grief, weeping and sobbing, so he could hardly tell me that mother had died in the night,"[4] she recalled. Edison had little time to grieve for Mary. He continued installing his electric light system in houses, companies, and even ships. It was a huge accomplishment, but Edison had even more ideas for the future.

Left: A picture of the first electric light bulb invented in 1879.

Right: A picture of the first electric lamp.

Both were invented by Thomas Edison and patented on January 27, 1880.

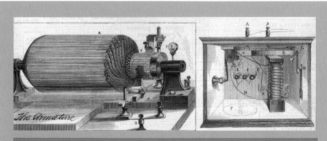

Edison was responsible for hundreds of inventions related to the creation and distribution of electricity. At left is Edison's armature, which was part of a generator. At right is one of his electric meters, which measure the amount of electricity.

Edward Bellamy and *Looking Backward*

One of the most important books published toward the end of the 19th century was Edward Bellamy's utopian novel Looking Backward.

In Looking Backward, *a young upper class Bostonian falls asleep in 1887 and wakes up in the year 2000. To his shock and surprise, the problems of hunger and poverty, which were rampant as the United States began industrializing in the 19th century, had been solved. The government had taken over all the major industries and ran them to benefit the entire society. Technology had also made life much easier. People who began their working lives at the age of 21 could retire at 45.*

Edward Bellamy

Looking Backward *was a huge bestseller and was translated into more than 20 languages. People did not just buy the book and read it. They formed Bellamy clubs and got involved in populist political movements.*

Bellamy was born in 1850 and raised in Chicopee, Massachusetts, by parents who were free-thinking Christians. As a young man he became very concerned about the state of American society and the often-harmful ways in which people treated each other. He became a newspaper writer and editor in hopes of improving society. He also tried to address current issues, such as poverty, through his fiction writing.

In 1886 workers at the McCormick Reaper Works in Chicago went on strike, or walked off the job together. They were demanding better working conditions, such as an eight-hour day. The strike turned violent when police shot at striking workers. Workers gathered at Haymarket Square the next day to protest police violence. A bomb was set off and seven police officers were killed.

Bellamy wrote Looking Backward *amidst growing concern about the negative effects of industrialization and the widening gulf between the rich and the poor. After the book was published, Bellamy went on a speaking tour around the country. He also began a new newspaper and worked on a sequel to* Looking Backward. *The sequel* Equality *was published in 1897. Bellamy died in 1898.*

Mina Miller was Edison's second wife. As Edison grew older, he became more willing to spend time with family and friends. But he remained hard-working and driven all his life.

5

Turning to Entertainment

After years of dedicating himself almost entirely to the project of electric light, in 1886 Edison decided to go back to work on his phonograph and also begin the effort to invent a motion picture machine. The previous year, he met and fell in love with Mina Miller. She was a well-educated 19-year-old woman whose family was involved in the founding of the Chautauqua Institution, a famous program of educational and cultural activities for adults. Mina was much younger than Edison and her family was unsure if she should marry him. But Edison worked hard at convincing them. The two were married on February 24, 1886. They would have three children: Madeleine, Charles, and Theodore.

Edison bought a beautiful mansion known as Glenmont near West Orange, New Jersey. He then built a large complex in West Orange that was designed for inventing and manufacturing. It contained a library, a laboratory, a machine shop, and experimentation rooms. Edison wanted to build the best private center for research in the world. He wrote, "I will have the best equipped & largest Laboratory extant, and the facilities incomparably superior to any other for rapid & cheap development of an invention, & working it up into commercial shape. . . ."[1]

Once the new facilities were built, Edison gave one of his employees, William Dickson, a secret assignment. Edison asked Dickson to

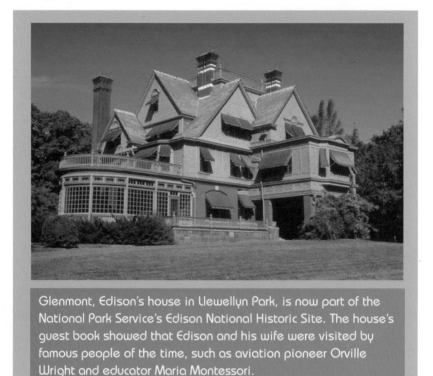

Glenmont, Edison's house in Llewellyn Park, is now part of the National Park Service's Edison National Historic Site. The house's guest book showed that Edison and his wife were visited by famous people of the time, such as aviation pioneer Orville Wright and educator Maria Montessori.

figure out how to film motion and then view the recorded images. Edison took a two-month trip to Europe in 1889 to see the sights and meet other inventors. The moment he returned, he hurried back to his laboratory to check on Dickson's progress. He sat down in a darkened room. He saw a cloudy image of Dickson raising his hat in greeting projected on a screen by a bulky machine. On a phonograph that sat next to the machine, Dickson's recorded voice said, "Good morning, Mr. Edison, glad to see you back. I hope you are satisfied with the Kineto-phonograph."[2]

Edison and Dickson still had much work to do to perfect the motion picture camera, but they had a good start. Edison worked hard to make the phonograph and the motion picture camera commercially successful. It was difficult to know the best way to create interest in the devices and sell them. Edison was a brilliant inventor and production engineer but he sometimes guessed wrong about the future of the entertainment industry. He thought the whole idea of using radios to hear music would die out because he did not think the technological problems could be overcome. He said, "There are several laws of nature which cannot be overcome when attempts are made to make the radio a musical instrument."[3]

In 1890 Edison launched a venture that was probably the closest he ever came to failing. He bought an old iron ore mine and began developing systems for getting more ore from the mine. Ten years later, Edison finally shut down the mine. He had come up with some good inventions and systems for mining, but the low price of iron never made the project worthwhile.

Edison then turned his attention to designing new and better batteries. He intended to build a battery that could power a car and thus make gas-burning engines unnecessary. That venture was also not a big success. It would take another century of driving gas-burning cars and the concerns over global warming to once again raise interest in cars fueled entirely by electricity.

While Edison went from one project to another, his reputation and the myths that surrounded him grew. Many stories and books exaggerated his skills. In one, Edison repelled an invasion from Mars with a "disintegrator" he had invented. His fame made it so he had to be careful about what he said. He caused a huge controversy in 1910 when he said he did not really believe in God and that he thought people were too religious. Partners in his many businesses begged him not to say anything else that would offend the vast church-going American public. Edison insisted that he had a right to publicly cast doubt on religion.

"I have never seen the slightest scientific proof of the religious theories of heaven and hell, of future life for individuals, or of a personal God. . . . I work on certain lines that might be called, perhaps, mechanical. . . . Proof! Proof! That is what I have always been after,"[4] Edison said.

At the age of 73, Edison began to slow down a little, but he still worked hard. He helped the government during World War II. In this picture, Edison is celebrating his birthday with his sons, Charles on the left and Thomas Jr. on the right.

As World War I approached, Edison volunteered to advise the government on inventions and discoveries that would help the war effort. His biggest contribution was finding ways to manufacture some key chemicals that were in short supply during the war. One of these was carbolic acid, which was used in making explosives. Once the war started, the supply from England was cut off. Edison designed and built a carbolic acid plant in 17 days, much quicker than the six months such a project would normally take.

As Edison grew older, he became more willing to take time off to relax and spend time with his family. He became good friends with

Edison struggled with being partially deaf all his life. But he sometimes saw his difficulty hearing as an asset. A device with sound, such as a telephone or a motion picture projector, had to work very well in order for him to be able to hear it.

Henry Ford, at left, takes Edison's hand. At right is Harvey Firestone, who founded an American tire empire, and was also friends with the two men. The three took frequent camping trips with other luminaries of the day, such as President Warren G. Harding.

Henry Ford, a founder of the American auto industry. The two men established winter homes near Fort Myers, Florida. The two homes are now combined into a museum that preserves the environment in which the men talked and worked on inventions and discoveries.

In his old age, Edison saw the need for new supplies of rubber. He experimented with thousands of plants until he had developed a goldenrod plant that grew 14 feet tall. It had a high concentration of latex, from which rubber could be made. His research was not put to commercial use because other scientists discovered a way to make artificial rubber.

Even when Edison struggled with illnesses such as diabetes as an elderly man, he was always the scientist. He treated the doctors' attempts to heal him with his usual scientific curiosity, suggesting that different treatments might serve as good experiments.

Thomas Alva Edison died on October 18, 1931. People all over the world showed their appreciation for him by simultaneously turning out their lights at 10 P.M. on the evening of the great man's funeral. Then they turned their lights right back on. In the lifetime of one man, the electric light had gone from being unthinkable to indispensable.

While Edison changed the way people lived in their homes by providing inexpensive electric light, his friend and contemporary, Henry Ford, changed the way people traveled by providing inexpensive automobiles.

French inventor Jean-Joseph-Étienne Lenoir designed the first internal combustion, or gas-burning, engine in 1859. Companies in Europe and the United States began building and selling cars throughout the late 19th century. But they produced the cars slowly and the prices were high.

Ford, who had worked as chief engineer for one of Edison's light companies, started his own car company in 1903. In 1908 he produced the first Model T. The genius of the Model T was that it could be mass-produced—many could be made at one time. It was also the first truly affordable car. At first it cost about $1,200, but by 1924 the price was down to $290.

Ford also paid his employees five dollars a day, which was a high salary for a manufacturing job in those days. He paid his employees well because he wanted them to be able to afford to buy a car for themselves. He also wanted to keep them from quitting the sometimes boring and repetitive assembly line work at the factory.

Ford pioneered the idea of paying factory workers a decent wage, but he refused to recognize the United Autoworkers Union (UAW) during the 1930s. By 1941, the Ford Motor Company was found to have violated the workers' rights by refusing to negotiate with the UAW. A major strike at Ford's biggest plant in River Rouge, Michigan, in 1941 finally led to the recognition of the union.

Ford died in 1947, leaving most of his huge estate—estimated at between $500 and $700 million—to the Ford Foundation, a non-profit organization that supports democracy, innovation, and the alleviation of poverty throughout the world.

Chronology

1847	Born on February 11 in Milan, Ohio
1854	Moves to Port Huron, Michigan
1859	Begins selling newspapers and other items on trains
1863	Begins working as telegrapher
1868	Discovers Michael Faraday's *Experimental Researches in Electricity* while working as a telegraph operator in Boston
1869	Quits working as a telegrapher to become a full-time inventor; receives his first recorded patent, for a vote-counting machine
1871	Opens a shop in Newark to manufacture stock tickers for Western Union; marries Mary Stilwell
1876	Finishes work on the quadruplex telegraph machine, which enables Western Union to send telegrams much faster
1877	Invents the phonograph, the first recording device, but puts it aside in favor of the light bulb
1879	Produces a light bulb, starts working on an electrical power system
1881	As investors look on, powers 425 lamps around Menlo Park for 12 hours using only a ton and a half of coal, which works out to less than a penny
1882	Lights up a small area of New York City in September
1884	Wife Mary dies
1886	Marries Mina Miller
1888	Designs commercially successful phonograph
1889	Works on the motion picture camera
1890	Buys iron ore mine and tries to make it commercially successful
1894	Presents the first movies in New York
1900	Closes his failed iron ore mine
1903	Unveils new, improved battery, only to withdraw it when it fails to measure up to his expectations
1909	Brings out new battery after many years of hard laboratory work
1915	Chairs a committee of scientists charged with helping the U.S. military during World War I
1928	Receives Medal of Honor from U.S. Congress to recognize his many useful inventions
1931	Dies on October 18 in West Orange, New Jersey, at the age of 84

Timeline of Discovery

1752 Benjamin Franklin demonstrates that lightning is electricity.

1808 Sir Humphry Davy creates a blue light by running an electric current across a small gap between two carbon rods.

1827 German physicist Georg Simon Ohm publishes his investigation into electrical currents, including what becomes known as Ohm's Law.

1831 British inventor Michael Faraday demonstrates that mechanical energy can be converted into electrical energy.

1835 Samuel F.B. Morse applies electrical currents to the sending letters – using a system of dots and dashes to represent letters.

1851 The Western Union Company is founded.

1863 Hermann Helmholtz, a German scientist, publishes a landmark study on the nature of sound and hearing.

1866 Steamship *Great Eastern* lays the first transatlantic telegraph cable.

1876 Alexander Graham Bell invents the telephone.

1895 Guglielmo Marconi invents wireless telegraph system.

1903 Orville and Wilbur Wright fly the first airplane.

1906 Henry Ford rolls out his Model N, the precursor to the Model T.

1915 D.W. Griffiths' Civil War epic movie *The Birth of a Nation* premieres.

1917 The United States enters World War I, declaring war against Germany.

1927 The Jazz Singer, starring Al Jolson, is the first "talkie" (movie with synchronized sound).

1929 The stock market collapse leads to the Great Depression.

1935 *Becky Sharp* is first successful color movie.

1939 World War II begins with the German invasion of Poland.

1945 The United States drops atomic bombs on the Japanese cities of Hiroshima and Nagasaki.

1948 The introduction of long-playing records (LPs) improves sound quality and makes it possible to record more music.

1958 The first American satellite is launched into orbit.

1969 Neil Armstrong becomes the first person to walk on the moon.

1975 The digital age begins with the invention of the personal computer.

2004 A year after the American war with Iraq, electricity shortage is still a major problem in Iraq.

Chapter Notes

Chapter One: Recording a Miracle
1. Matthew Josephson, *Edison: A Biography* (New York: McGraw-Hill Book Company, 1959), p. 163.
2. Ibid.

Chapter Two: Growing up Inventive
1. Paul Israel, *Edison: A Life of Invention* (New York: John Wiley & Sons, Inc., 1998), p. 8.
2. Ibid., p. 7.

Chapter Three: Becoming an Inventor
1. William H. Meadowcroft, *The Boys' Life of Edison* (New York: Harper & Row, 1911), p. 43.
2. Matthew Josephson, *Edison: A Biography* (New York: McGraw-Hill Book Company Inc., 1959), p. 63.
3. Ibid., p. 99.
4. Ibid.
5. Paul Israel, *Edison: A Life of Invention* (New York: John Wiley & Sons, Inc., 1998), p. 131.
6. Josephson, p. 326.

Chapter Four: Lighting up the World
1. Francis Jehl, *Menlo Park Reminiscences* (Dearborn, Michigan: Edison Institute, 1936), p. 217.
2. Matthew Josephson, *Edison: A Biography* (New York: McGraw-Hill Book Company, 1959), p. 186.
3. Paul Israel, *Edison: A Life of Invention* (New York: John Wiley & Sons, Inc., 1998), p. 192.
4. Josephson, p. 290.

Chapter Five: Turning to Entertainment
1. Paul Israel, *Edison: A Life of Invention* (New York: John Wiley & Sons, Inc., 1998), p. 260.
2. Matthew Josephson, *Edison: A Biography* (New York: McGraw-Hill Book Company, 1959), p. 338.
3. Israel, p. 456.
4. Josephson, p. 438.

Glossary

cylinder
(SILL-uhn-dur)—a round, tubular object with flat circular ends.

enlightenment
(in-LIE-ten-ment)—a time of increased learning and understanding.

entrepreneur
(AHN-truh-prun-uhr)—a person who starts his or her own business.

incandescent
(in-can-DEH-sent)—bright light created by electricity.

induction
(in-DUCK-shun)– the creation of electric energy from magnetism.

patent
(PAT-unt)—a document issued by the government that gives an inventor the exclusive right to use the invention.

platinum
(PLA-tin-uhm)—a type of metal that is more valuable than gold and resistant to electricity.

populist
(POP-you-list)—a person in favor of ordinary people.

rebellion
(ree-BELL-ee-un)—a fight or struggle against an authority.

For Further Reading

For Young Adults

Adair, Gene. *Thomas Alva Edison: Inventing the Electric Age.* New York: Oxford University Press, 1996.

Delano, Marfé Ferguson. *Inventing the Future: A Photobiography of Thomas Alva Edison.* Washington, D.C.: National Geographic, 2002.

Guthridge, Sue. *Thomas Edison: Young Inventor.* New York: Aladdin Books, 1986.

Sullivan, George. *Thomas Edison.* New York: Scholastic, 2002.

Van de Water, Marjorie. *Edison Experiments You Can Do.* New York: Harper and Brothers, 1960.

Works Consulted

Baldwin, Neil. *Edison: Inventing the Century.* New York: Hyperion, 1995.

Conot, Robert. *A Streak of Luck: The Life and Legend of Thomas Alva Edison.* New York: Simon and Schuster, 1979.

Israel, Paul. *Edison: A Life of Invention.* New York: John Wiley & Sons, Inc., 1998.

Jehl, Francis. *Menlo Park Reminiscences.* Dearborn, Michigan: Edison Institute, 1936.

Josephson, Matthew. *Edison: A Biography.* New York: McGraw-Hill Book Company Inc., 1959.

Meadowcroft, William H. *The Boys' Life of Edison.* New York: Harper & Row, 1911.

On the Internet

The Edison National Historic Site
http://www.nps.gov/edis

Thomas A. Edison Papers, Rutgers University
http://edison.rutgers.edu/taep.htm

Edison Birthplace Museum
http://www.tomedison.org

Greenfield Village at The Henry Ford
http://www.hfmgv.org/village/edisonatwork.asp

Edison Winter Home and Museum
http://www.edison-ford-estate.com

Index